SONATA NO. 3 IN A MINOR
Antonio Vivaldi
transcribed and edited for bass tuba and piano by
R. Winston Morris

about the composer

Antonio Vivaldi was born circa 1675 in Venice, Italy, and died in Venice in 1741. He was a priest and a prolific composer.

Vivaldi's genius is recognized primarily in his instrumental works. Many of J.S. Bach's compositions were fashioned after Vivaldi's numerous concerti.

about the music

SONATA NO. 3 IN A MINOR was most likely written for violoncello and has been arranged or transcribed for many instruments.

rehearsal and performance suggestions

The dotted rhythms in the first movement must be absolutely precise. Baroque trills start *above* the written note.

The second movement is basically light and should be played with a slight "bouncy" rhythm.

Let the lyrical third movement sing and be certain the dotted rhythm is not played like the triplet rhythm.

The fourth movement must be precise in terms of pitch placement, articulation and dynamics.

All repeats are optional and metronome markings serve only as guidelines.

/s/ R. Winston Morris

about the transcriber

R. Winston Morris is Professor of Music at Tennessee Technological University in Cookeville, Tennessee. He is Coordinator of the Brass Division at Tech and Director of the Brass Choir. In 1967 he founded the now internationally recognized Tenn Tech Tuba Ensemble, a pioneering ensemble which has toured extensively throughout the eastern half of the United States. Mr. Morris holds degrees from East Carolina University and Indiana University where he was a student of William J. Bell. He is considered one of the leading authorities on the literature for the tuba, having authored the widely used *Tuba Music Guide*. A former president of the Tubist Universal Brotherhood Association, Mr. Morris is considered one of the founding fathers of that organization. He presently performs with the Chamber Brass Quintet, a faculty ensemble in residence at Tech, and the Matteson-Phillips Tubajazz Consort.

The Publisher

duration: approximately 9½ minutes, without repeats

Tuba and Piano Parts (LA194)   Extra Tuba Parts (LC940)   Extra Piano Parts (LC939)

Shawnee Press

EXCLUSIVELY DISTRIBUTED BY

HAL•LEONARD® CORPORATION

7777 W. BLUEMOUND RD. P.O. BOX 13819 MILWAUKEE, WI 53213

T0056131

SONATA NO. 3 IN A MINOR

Antonio Vivaldi
transcribed and edited for bass tuba and piano by
R. Winston Morris

4

SONATA NO. 3 IN A MINOR

Tuba

Antonio Vivaldi
transcribed and edited for bass tuba and piano by
R. Winston Morris